THINK SPOTS

FOR LIFE

A MOMENT OF REFLECTION
TO GIVE YOU DIRECTION

Conceived, Noticed and Compiled by

DERRIC JOHNSON

OUTCOME
PUBLISHING

Think Spots for Life

Published by Outcome Publishing
8007 18th Avenue West
Bradenton, Florida 34209
www.outcomepublishing.com

First Edition

Printed in the United States of America

1. Religion: Spiritual General
2. Self-Help: Spiritual
3. Religion: Christian Life – Personal Growth

Dedicated to my daughter, Jaci,
who inspired this book...
and to my wife, Debbie, who gave me Jaci.

FOREWARD

Jaci Jo (officially christened Jaclyn Joelle Johnson) is daughter number four of our five children. I'm not sure how one older brother slipped in there, but I'm very glad he did... kind of balances out the home front hormones.

Jaci and I were very close as she grew up. Since she came late in my life, I knew there would be no more parental chances, and I determined to make the most of this opportunity. (Nature makes fathers... but nurture creates Daddies.)

When she was four years old, we started enjoying weekly "date nights" while Mommy was busy with "lady church-stuff." We would split a meal at a restaurant of her choice... and then shop for computer games.

She had her first start-up computer right in my office so we could laugh, chat and dream together. (I still have in my files all of her best lines and definitions... treasure to this day.)

I determined that nothing would get in the way of our times together... it was that important to me. More than once I would be on my way to a meeting, coat and tie on, briefcase in hand, and she would stop me for a very important conversation. I'd put the briefcase down, whisper to Debbie, "Call ahead and tell them I'll be 10 minutes late."

Jaci stunned me one Father's Day with a picture booklet of us... and one of her comments was MY DADDY IS A VERY BUSY MAN...BUT HE ALWAYS HAS TIME FOR ME. (Glad she noticed.)

Then she went away to Lee University in Cleveland, Tennessee... and basically disappeared. My little girl got so caught up in college life she wouldn't phone or write... or even email. Debbie could get a response once in a while by texting, "Are you eating well... and are you healthy?" The answer would come back in one terse word... YES.

That really didn't satisfy a lonely Daddy… so one day I cut a ten dollar bill in half and mailed it to her with a short note attached, "When you call… the other half of this bill will be in the mail." It wasn't long until the phone rang and I heard her voice say… DADDY. After I put down the receiver, I looked at Debbie and remarked, "Well, that worked… but it's gonna be expensive to keep that up."

I wasn't going to be a pesky parent and call her all the time. That would be way over the top. I told Debbie, "If I can just touch her every day, I can live happy." So that's when these THINK SPOTS were born. Every morning I send an email to her with something humorous, or motivating, or challenging, or faith-building. Often these "spontaneous spots" hit her just right with some truth she needs for settling and focus. (More than once she has posted a TS on her face book page with the caption, "Sometimes I think my Father may be the smartest man in the universe."

Jaci and I have been at this for three years now (there are over a thousand) and lots of people have asked to be included in the daily mailings. But some of the THINK SPOTS are by design, "up close and personal," so I picked out 365… a whole year's worth. And I'll sign them for you just like I do for her every day,

"I LOVE YOU FROM THE BOTTOM OF MY HEART TO THE TOP OF YOUR DREAMS."

For her I sign DADDY…

but for you I'm

DERRIC JOHNSON

CONTENTS

FAMILY

Home is an
attic full of yesterday,
a hope chest full of tomorrow
surrounded by the four walls of today.

FAMILY

Nature makes a Father…
Nurture makes a Dad.

A mother holds her children's hands for a
while…but holds their hearts forever.

**A HOUSE IS MADE OF
WALLS AND BEAMS…
BUT A HOME IS BUILT
OF LOVE AND DREAMS.**

A TRULY RICH MAN IS ONE
WHOSE CHILDREN RUN INTO HIS ARMS...
WHEN HIS HANDS ARE EMPTY.

Parents who are lucky in the
kind of children they have...
have children who are lucky
in the kind of parents they have.

Life doesn't come with
an instruction book...
that's why we have fathers.

11

Travel for excitement…
come home for love.

FATHERS ARE WHAT
GIVE DAUGHTERS AWAY
TO OTHER MEN
WHO AREN'T NEARLY
GOOD ENOUGH
SO THEY CAN HAVE
GRANDCHILDREN
SMARTER THAN ANYBODY'S.

*It's easier for a father to have a child…
than it is for a child to have a father.*

DAD... THE LOCAL BRANCH OF THE MONEY TREE.

We need 4 hugs a day for survival.
We need 8 hugs a day for maintenance.
We need 12 hugs a day for growth.

It is not easy to be
crafty and winsome
at the same time…
and few there be
who accomplish it
after the age of six.

About the only two things a young
child will share willingly...
are contagious diseases
and parental secrets.

To train children at home,
it's necessary for both parents and children...
to spend some time there.

MOST OF US GROW UP

AND GET MARRIED...

BUT NOT NECESSARILY IN THAT ORDER.

A MAN CAN SAY ANYTHING HE PLEASES IN HIS OWN HOME. NOBODY'S LISTENING ANYWAY.

Give a kid an inch…
he wants to become a ruler.

It isn't what a teen-ager
knows that worries
his parents.
It's how he found out.

SILENCE IS GOLDEN...
UNLESS YOU HAVE CHILDREN.
THEN SILENCE IS SUSPICIOUS.

Good Moms let you lick the beater batter.
Great Moms turn them off first.

I'm not afraid of anything.
I have daughters.

FRIENDS

Angels exist…
But sometimes they
don't have wings,
So we call them friends.

FRIENDS

Some people know how to
live everyone's life…
but their own.

THOSE WHO DESERVE LOVE
THE LEAST…
NEED IT THE MOST.

Forgiveness does not
change the past…
but it does enlarge the future.

PEOPLE CAN'T DRIVE YOU CRAZY...
IF YOU DON'T GIVE THEM THE KEYS.

Who means the most to you...
says the most about you.

A true friend…
stabs you in the front.

The only way to
multiply happiness...
is to divide it.

**A FRIEND IS SOMEONE
WHO ASKS HOW YOU ARE...
AND THEN WAITS
TO HEAR THE ANSWER.**

*A friend hears
the song in your heart...
and then sings it to you
when your memory fails.*

THE SMALLEST
ACT OF KINDNESS
IS WORTH MORE...
THAN THE
GRANDEST INTENTION.

SOMETIMES...

TWO IS A CROWD.

Write injuries in dust...
benefits in marble.

Cooperation is the conviction
that nobody can get there…
unless everybody gets there.

There are times
when silence…
has a
voice of its own.

Friendship is
like a bank account…
you can't continue
to draw on it
without making deposits.

**A FRIEND OVERLOOKS
YOUR BROKEN FENCE. . .
AND ADMIRES YOUR GARDEN.**

**IT IS EASIER TO FORGIVE PEOPLE
FOR MAKING MISTAKES...
THAN FOR WITNESSING OURS.**

*Love is a peculiar thing.
In order to get it, you have to give it.
And when you get it…
you have to give it back to keep it.*

23

LOVE
WILL FIND A WAY...
INDIFFERENCE
WILL FIND AN EXCUSE.

Love never asks
how much must I do...
but how can I do it.

LIFE IS MEASURED
BY MOMENTS IN TIME ...
LOVE IS MEASURED
BY TIMELESS MOMENTS.

Love is like
an hourglass
with the
heart filling up
as the brain empties.

**FOR NEWS
OF THE HEART...
ASK THE FACE.**

*People who throw kisses...
are hopelessly lazy.*

Age does not protect you from love... but love, to some extent, protects you from age.

Love is friendship
that caught fire.

Keep positive with your friends.
No one has enough
armor to withstand
a constant barrage
of CAN'T and WON'T.

MEN USUALLY LOVE WOMEN
FOR WHAT THEY ARE.
WOMEN USUALLY LOVE MEN
FOR WHAT THEY MIGHT BE.

TRUCE IS BETTER THAN FRICTION.

I dislike the guys
who criticize
the other guys
whose enterprise
has made them rise
above the guys
who criticize.

27

HITTING THE KID
WITH THE BALL
MIGHT GET YOU THE BALL...
BUT IT WON'T
GET YOU ANYONE
TO THROW IT TO.

You are my favorite
HELLO…
and my hardest
GOODBYE.

FORTITUDE

Everything will be fine
in the end.
If it isn't fine...
then it isn't the end.

FORTITUDE

On the highway of life…
there are many a flattened squirrel
who couldn't make a decision.

SOMETIMES THE THINGS
THAT ARE HARDEST FOR US...
ARE THE THINGS
WE NEED TO DO THE MOST.

Opportunities are usually disguised as hard work...
so most people don't recognize them.

Challenges are
what make life interesting...
overcoming them
is what makes life meaningful.

NEVER LOOK AT

WHAT YOU HAVE LOST...

ALWAYS LOOK AT

WHAT YOU HAVE LEFT.

*The person who has a WHY to live...
can bear almost any HOW.*

Whatever you do, give 100%...
unless it's donating blood.

Don't be a "middle of the roader."
There's nothing
in the middle of the road...
except yellow stripes and dead
armadillos.

**NOTHING IS SO EXHAUSTING
AS INDECISION...
AND NOTHING SO FUTILE.**

When I was five years old my mother
told me that happiness was the key to life.
When I got to school they asked me
what I wanted to be when I grew up.
I wrote down, "Happy."
They said I didn't understand the assignment.
I said they didn't understand life.

ALWAYS BE THE PERSON WHO
FINDS JOY EVERYWHERE HE GOES…
AND LEAVES IT BEHIND HIM
WHEN HE LEAVES.

Attitudes are contagious
and from time to time
we need to ask ourselves…
"Is mine worth catching?"

33

RING THE BELLS
THAT STILL CAN RING.
FORGET YOUR
PERFECT OFFERING.
THERE IS A
CRACK IN EVERYTHING...
THAT'S HOW
THE LIGHT GETS IN.

Never believe that a few caring
people can't change the world.
Actually... that's all who ever have.

IMPRESSION WITHOUT EXPRESSION...
LEADS TO DEPRESSION.

It's never crowded...
along the extra mile.

**One of these day…
is none of these days.**

SOME PEOPLE
ARE LIKE BLISTERS...
THEY DON'T SHOW UP
UNTIL THE WORK IS DONE.

HAM AND EGGS...
For the chicken
it's all in a day's work.
But for the pig
it's a lifetime commitment.

The stronger the wind blows...
the higher your kite will fly.

THE ONLY PLACE THAT
SUCCESS COMES BEFORE WORK...
IS IN THE DICTIONARY.

DON'T JUST COUNT THE DAYS...
MAKE THE DAYS COUNT.

For all that has been...THANKS.
For all that shall be...YES!

The steam that
blows the whistle…
cannot be used
to turn the wheels.

37

THE TRUE MEANING OF LIFE
IS TO PLANT TREES...
UNDER WHOSE SHADE
YOU DO NOT EXPECT TO SIT.

What is right is often forgotten…
when it is replaced
by what is convenient.

Being good is commendable...
but only when it is combined
with doing good is it useful.

We need to do what we can do...
and let God do what we cannot.

It is the service
we are not
obliged to give...
that people value most.

**DON'T TRY TOO HARD
TO FIT IN...
YOU WERE CREATED
TO STAND OUT.**

Do more than belong... participate.
Do more than care... help.
Do more than believe... practice.
Do more than be fair... be kind.
Do more than forgive... forget.
Do more than dream... work.

Don't be afraid
to take small steps...
there's something powerful
about momentum.

BE YOURSELF...

EVERYONE ELSE IS TAKEN.

FAITH

Faith is not belief
without proof...
It is trust
without reservation.

FAITH

The Bible was not written
to satisfy your curiosity...
it was written
to transform your life.

WORRY ABOUT NOTHING.

PRAY ABOUT EVERYTHING.

Be sure you sins will find you OUCH.

TO SEE THE SEEDS IN AN APPLE...
THAT IS REALITY.
TO SEE THE APPLES IN A SEED...
THAT IS VISION.

The task ahead of you
is never as great…
as the God within you.

Any concern too small
to be turned into a prayer...
is too small
to be made into a burden.

Trust God...
but row away
from the rocks.

**We must pray
with our eyes on God…
not on the difficulties.**

GOD LOVES
EACH OF US...
AS IF THERE
WERE ONLY ONE OF US.

GOD'S WILL
IS NOT AN ITINERARY...
IT'S AN ATTITUDE.

All that I have seen
teaches me...
to trust the Creator
for all I have not seen.

*It's better to stand with God
and be judged by the world...
than to stand with the world
and be judged by God.*

45

He who
kneels down to God...
can stand up
to anybody.

FAITH IS TRUSTING GOD...
WHEN KNOWLEDGE IS NOT AVAILABLE.

Faith has less to do
with gaining knowledge...
and more to do with
causing wonder.

Before we can pray,
"Lord, Thy kingdom come,"
we must be willing to pray,
"My kingdom go."

FAITH SEES THE INVISIBLE...
BELIEVES THE INCREDIBLE...
RECEIVES THE IMPOSSIBLE!

KNOW IN YOUR HEART
THAT ALL THINGS
ARE POSSIBLE.

We couldn't
conceive of a miracle…
if none ever happened.

NEVER
DOUBT IN THE DARK…
WHAT GOD SHOWED YOU
IN THE LIGHT.

With God…
all things are possible.
Without God…
all things are permissible.

THE BEST CURE FOR WOBBLY KNEES...
IS TO KNEEL ON THEM.

God loves you because
of who He is...
not because of anything
you did or didn't do.

WHEN YOU HAVE EVERYTHING...
FAITH IS NOTHING.
WHEN YOU HAVE NOTHING...
FAITH IS EVERYTHING.

*Sometimes the Lord takes us
into troubled waters...
not to drown us but to cleanse us.*

If God died...
how long would it take you to notice?

Without God
your week would be...
Mournday
Tearsday
Wasteday
Thirstday
Frightday
Sadderday
Sinday

**When you know who your God is…
you can plant in a famine.**

GOD'S WILL IS LIKE
THE RUDDER ON A SHIP…
TOTALLY INACTIVE
UNTIL THE SHIP MOVES.

You supply the motion…
God provides the direction.
Proverbs 3:5-6

EVERY TIME I PASS A CHURCH,
I STOP TO PAY A VISIT;
LEST SOME DAY WHEN
I'M CARRIED THERE,
THE LORD WON'T SAY,
"WHO IS IT?"

Satan wants you to stay home from
church when it rains ...
he knows dry people burn better.

FUN

Knowledge is knowing
that a tomato is a fruit.
Wisdom is not putting
a tomato in a fruit salad.

FUN

How long is a minute?
It depends on what side of the
bathroom door you're on.

**If Walmart is
lowering prices every day…
how come nothing is free yet?**

A mentor told me, to achieve inner peace
is to finish what I start.
So far today I finished
two bags of M&Ms and a chocolate cake.
I feel better already.

EXPECTING LIFE TO TREAT YOU WELL
BECAUSE YOU ARE A GOOD PERSON...
IS LIKE EXPECTING
AN ANGRY BULL NOT TO CHARGE
BECAUSE YOU ARE A VEGETARIAN.

Women and cats will do as they please.
Men and dogs
should just relax and get used to it.

IF THE FIRST THING
YOU DO WHEN YOU WAKE UP
IN THE MORNING
IS EAT A LIVE FROG...
THEN NOTHING WORSE
CAN HAPPEN
FOR THE REST OF THE DAY.

I CAN QUIT CHOCOLATE
ANYTIME...
BUT I'M NO QUITTER.

Some minds are like concrete...
thoroughly mixed up and permanently set.

Even if life is
all peaches and cream...
you still have to watch out
for pits and cholesterol.

There's a difference in
having an open mind…
and having a hole in your head.

THE CAFFEINE IN COFFEE IS GOOD…
IT ALLOWS YOU TO DO
STUPID THINGS WITH MORE ENERGY.

"ALL I NEED IS A
DEEP FAITH IN GOD…
AND A
STRONG CUP OF COFFEE."

Watch out when you're getting all you want...
only hogs being fattened
for slaughter get all they want.

Patience is
keeping cool as a cucumber...
when the rest of the world
is going bananas.

WISE MEN TALK BECAUSE
THEY HAVE SOMETHING TO SAY...
FOOLS TALK BECAUSE
THEY HAVE TO SAY SOMETHING.

**NEVER SHARE YOUR PROBLEMS
WITH OTHER PEOPLE.
MOST OF THEM WON'T CARE...
AND THE REST WILL BE GLAD.**

Some people are like Slinkies.
Not good for anything...
but they put a smile on your face
when you push them
down the stairs.

MY MIND NOT ONLY WANDERS...

SOMETIMES IT

JUST LEAVES COMPLETELY.

59

**Happiness is not measured by wealth.
For instance, a man with $8,000,000
may not be a bit happier…
than a man with $7,000,000.**

Happiness is like jam...
you can't spread even a little
without getting some on yourself.

A good memory test
is to sit down...
and recall the things
that you worried about
at this time last year.

A Sunday School teacher looked up from
reading her Bible
and asked the class,
"What do you think a land flowing with
milk and honey would be like?"
Answered one little boy, "Sticky!"

SOME FOLKS NEVER SEEM
TO HEAR WHAT YOU SAY…
EXCEPT WHEN YOU'RE SAYING IT
TO SOMEONE ELSE.

Every household should
have a filing cabinet…
upon which to stack important papers.

You do have to admire one thing
about TV sitcom families...
they never waste time
watching television.

The toughest part of dieting isn't
watching what you eat...
it's watching what your friends eat.

**Never take a
cross-country car trip…
with a kid who has
just learned to whistle.**

*Those who think that
the competitive spirit is dead...
ought to watch the customers
in a supermarket
when a cashier opens a new checkout lane.*

"I always get to the airport
an hour early.
That way, I can be one of the
first to know
that the flight has been delayed."

*"My kid is going to college as
part of a work-study program...
I work, he studies."*

"They make the
perfect couple.
He's a pill and
she's a headache."

"I LIKE MY DENTIST
BECAUSE HE'S QUICK...
DRILL, FILL AND BILL."

"It's amazing to see
the number of persons...
taking ego trips
with so little luggage."

An optimist believes
we live in the best of all possible worlds.
The pessimist fears
this is true.

PAPER IS ALWAYS STRONGEST
AT THE PERFORATIONS.

THE LION AND THE LAMB
SHALL LIE DOWN
TOGETHER...
BUT THE LAMB
WON'T GET MUCH SLEEP.

The shortest distance
between two points…
is always under construction.

There are two types of dirt...
the dark kind, attracted to light objects
and the light kind, attracted to dark objects.

The probability
of someone watching you...
is proportionate to
the stupidity of your actions.

FINANCES

A budget is a blueprint…
that shows you exactly which drain
your money is going down.

FINANCES

Money isn't everything…
according to those who have it.

GOD IS THE OWNER…
AND YOU ARE THE OWER.

THE LORD LOVETH
A CHEERFUL GIVER. . .
HE ALSO ACCEPTETH
FROM A GROUCH.

MONEY IS WHAT
THINGS RUN INTO...
AND PEOPLE RUN OUT OF.

Money is often confused with dough.
This is incorrect...
because dough sticks to your fingers.

IF YOUR OUTGO

EXCEEDS YOUR INCOME...

YOUR UPKEEP

WILL BECOME YOUR DOWNFALL.

WE JUST GOT A NEW TELEVISION SET
THAT IS THREE DIMENSIONAL.
IT GIVES US HEIGHT, WIDTH AND DEBT.

Money no longer talks.
It just goes without saying.

MONEY ISN'T
EVERYTHING.
FOR INSTANCE,
IT ISN'T
PLENTIFUL.

MONEY... WHAT IT IS
Workers earn it
Spendthrifts burn it
Bankers lend it
Women spend it
Forgers fake it
Taxes take it
Dying leave it
Heirs receive it
Thrifty save it
Misers crave it
Robbers seize it
Rich increase it
Gamblers lose it
I could use it

**NOWADAYS PEOPLE FIND THEMSELVES
LIVING IN MORE EXPENSIVE HOUSES...
AND THEY HAVEN'T EVEN MOVED!**

There are bigger things than money.
For instance, bills.

A nickel goes
a long way these days.
You can carry it around for weeks
before you find
something to buy with it.

Wealthy people miss
one of life's great thrills...
making the last car payment.

At our deli, inflation is a sign of the time:
Pumpernickel has become Pumperdime.

THE BEST THINGS
IN LIFE ARE FREE...
IT'S THE WORST THINGS
THAT ARE SO EXPENSIVE.

FIRST I GAVE UP MEAT

FOR LENT.

NOW I'M GIVING IT UP

FOR RENT.

MOST PEOPLE CONSIDER BUDGETING. . .
TO BE A FATE WORSE THAN DEBT.

Nothing seems to bring on
an emergency as quickly…
as putting money aside
in case of one.

FUTURE

Life without a dream
is like a hamburger without onions…
it just doesn't stick with you.

FUTURE

THE BEST PREPARATION FOR TOMORROW... IS THE RIGHT USE OF TODAY.

Turn your can'ts into cans...
And your dreams into plans.

**If opportunity isn't knocking...
build another door.**

THE HEART CAN
DISCERN MORE...
THAN THE EAR
CAN PERCEIVE.

At the edge
of my comfort zone...
Is where my life begins.

TIME FLIES...

IT'S UP TO YOU

TO BE THE NAVIGATOR.

**VISION WITHOUT ACTION
IS DAYDREAM.
ACTION WITHOUT VISION
IS NIGHTMARE.**

*If you wait until
all the lights are green
before you leave home…
you'll never
get started on your journey.*

**It may cost
a lot to dream…
but it costs
everything not to.**

WHERE HOPE GROWS...
MIRACLES BLOSSOM.

You can survive
without a dream...
but you cannot live
without a dream.

Tomorrow
is a clean slate...
limited only
by your imagination.

Forget about
pursuing your dream...
the idea is to catch it.

If you want
your dreams to come true...
the first thing you have to do is
WAKE UP!

Dreams come true...
One opportunity
at a time.

TO GET ANYWHERE...
START OUT
FOR SOMEWHERE...
OR YOU'LL GO NOWHERE.

We all live under the same sky...
but we don't all have
the same horizon.

A DREAM IS A WISH...
THAT WON'T GO AWAY.

The person who dares nothing…
need hope for nothing.

THE OPPORTUNITY OF A LIFETIME MUST BE SEIZED… DURING THE LIFETIME OF THE OPPORTUNITY.

While you stand there deciding
whether or not
to get your net…
the butterfly is flying away.

DREAMS ALWAYS COME
A SIZE TOO BIG. . .
SO YOU CAN
GROW INTO THEM.

EVERYTHING STARTS...
AS SOMEONE'S DAYDREAM.

LIMITS EXIST
ONLY IN THE SOULS...
OF THOSE
WHO DO NOT DREAM.

Be patient...
in time
the grass
becomes milk.

**You can't
get anywhere today...
if you are still
mired down in yesterday.**

If you are feeling confused,
maybe you are pulling
on the door marked PUSH.

When in doubt…
just take the next small step.

IF YOU'VE GOT A PULSE…
YOU'VE GOT A PURPOSE.

*Success is
not easy
and it's certainly
not for
the lazy.*

It's better to
aim at the stars
and miss
than to aim at the ground
and hit.

WHAT THE CATERPILLAR
CALLS THE END...
THE BUTTERFLY
CALLS THE BEGINNING.

Missing out is worse...
than messing up.

LOOK AT LIFE THROUGH
THE WINDSHIELD...
NOT THE REARVIEW MIRROR.

YOU DON'T HAVE to SEE
the WHOLE STAIRCASE. . .
YOU JUST HAVE
to tAKE the FIRSt StEP.

IF YOU ARE
GOING TO DREAM...
DREAM BIG!

Never let anyone or anything
define your value...
or limit your dream.

You can "how?"
a great idea...
right out the door.

Jump...
The net will appear!

GOD IS THE DREAM GIVER...
WE ARE THE DREAM BUILDERS.

IF YOU CAN'T SEE IT

BEFORE YOU SEE IT

YOU'LL NEVER SEE IT.

Neither a wise man
nor a brave man
lays down on the
tracks of history...
to wait for the train
of the future to run over him.

ONE DAY AND SOME DAY...

ARE NOT DAYS OF THE WEEK.

GET SPECIFIC.

WE DO NOT
SEE THINGS
AS THEY ARE.
WE SEE THINGS
AS WE ARE.

There are no
hopeless situations ...
only people who
think hopelessly.

Vision is hope
with a blueprint.

Only those who
see the invisible...
can do the impossible.

**EVEN IF YOU CAN'T
TAKE A FLYING LEAP. . .
TRY A LITTLE HOP
ONCE IN A WHILE.**

**If you wait
until you're really sure…
you'll never
take off the training wheels.**

EVERY MIGHTY KING
WAS ONCE A CRYING BABY.
EVERY GREAT TREE
WAS ONCE A TINY SEED.
EVERY TALL BUILDING
WAS ONCE ON PAPER.
SO IT IS WITH YOUR DREAM.

FIDELITY

If you have integrity…
nothing else matters.
If you don't have integrity…
nothing else matters.

FIDELITY

A bad attitude and a flat tire are alike.
Won't get you anywhere...
until it's changed.

ɕ

'I WANT MY LIFE...

TO BE MORE THAN LONG.

The measure of character
is not what comes from ancestors...
but what is left to descendants.

WHEN A LITTLE SUCCESS
TURNS SOMEONE'S HEAD. . .
IT INVARIABLY CAUSES
A PAIN IN THE NECK TO OTHER PEOPLE.

YOU CAN SMELL

THE COMPLIMENTS...

JUST DON'T INHALE THEM.

WE JUDGE OURSELVES
BY OUR INTENTIONS...
THE REST OF THE WORLD
JUDGES US BY OUR ACTIONS.

**It's not
where you start…
it's where
you finish that counts.**

You may be
disappointed if you fail…
but you are
doomed if you don't try.

None are so empty…
as those who are
full of themselves.

NO ONE CAN MAKE YOU FEEL INFERIOR... WITHOUT YOUR CONSENT.

IT IS NOT HAPPINESS
THAT MAKES US GRATEFUL...
BUT GRATEFULNESS
THAT MAKES US HAPPY.

Being good is commendable…
but only when it is
combined with doing good
is it useful.

Positive anything...
is better than
negative nothing.

ACT AS IF WHAT YOU DO
MAKES A DIFFERENCE.
IT DOES.

Life isn't about
finding yourself...
It's about
creating yourself.

What you leave behind
is not what is engraved
in stone monuments…
but what is woven
into the lives of others.

COURAGE IS NOT
THE ABSENCE OF FEAR…
BUT RATHER THE JUDGEMENT THAT
SOMETHING ELSE IS MORE IMPORTANT
THAN FEAR.

IT'S MORE IMPORTANT
TO BE NICE…
THAN IT IS
TO BE RIGHT.

WHAT WE ARE
IS GOD'S GIFT tO US...
WHAT WE BECOME
IS OUR GIFT tO GOD.

There is no better
test of your integrity…
than your behavior
when you are wrong.

TOO MANY PEOPLE
OVERVALUE
WHAT THEY ARE NOT...
AND UNDERVALUE
WHAT THEY ARE.

PLANT YOUR OWN GARDEN
AND DECORATE YOUR OWN SOUL...
INSTEAD OF WAITING FOR SOMEONE
TO BRING YOU FLOWERS.

*It's right to be content
with what you have...
but wrong to be content
with what you are.*

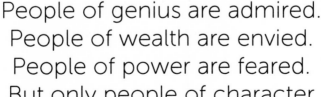

People of genius are admired.
People of wealth are envied.
People of power are feared.
But only people of character
are trusted.

What's the difference
between ignorance and apathy?
I don't know
and I don't care.

YOU ONLY LIVE ONCE...

BUT IF YOU DO IT RIGHT,

ONCE IS ENOUGH.

Do something today...
that your future self
will thank you for.

Note to daughter on her
first day of a new job:

Dress like a girl.
Act like a lady.
Think like a man.
Work like a boss.

Give God behavior...
He can bless.

THIS IS YOUR WORLD.
SHAPE IT...
OR SOMEONE ELSE WILL.

If you worry about your reputation...
you'll compromise your character.
Worry instead about your character.

PLAN THE BEST YOU CAN.
BE THE BEST YOU CAN.
DO THE BEST YOU CAN.

I'M NOT AFRAID

OF STORMS...

THAT'S HOW I LEARN

TO SAIL MY SHIP.

As we express our gratitude
we must never forget...
the highest appreciation
is not to utter words
but to live by them.

Aspire to
inspire
before you
expire.

WHATEVER YOUR
LOT IN LIFE...
BUILD SOMETHING
ON IT.

*It's more important
to be significant...
than it is to be relevant.*

Until you make peace with who you are...
you'll never be content with what you have.

**ONLY GOD CAN MAKE
FLOWERS AND TREES...
I AM IN CHARGE OF
SEEDS AND WEEDS.**

Never cease
to be amazed...
at the strength
of your weaknesses.

IT'S NOT WHO YOU KNOW...

IT'S WHO YOU ARE.

BE EARLY IF YOU'RE THE BIRD. . .
BE LATE IF YOU'RE THE WORM.

What you see
is what you get...
except in
pre-packaged strawberries.

FOCUS

Excellence is never an accident.

FOCUS

IT'S NOT HOW MUCH TIME YOU HAVE... IT IS HOW MUCH YOU USE.

A RIVER WITHOUT BANKS... IS JUST A BIG PUDDLE.

What most of us need
is a good swift kick…
in the seat of the can'ts.

IT'S NEVER TOO LATE TO BE. . .
WHO YOU MIGHT HAVE BEEN.

Always be curious.
Knowledge will
never seek you...
you must acquire it.

**YOU CANNOT COPY
THE TECHNIQUE
WITHOUT COPYING
THE PHILOSOPHY.**

EXCELLENCE IS WHERE PASSION MEETS PRECISION.

EFFICIENCY
is doing things right.
EFFECTIVENESS
is doing right things.
EXCELLENCE
is doing right things right.

THERE'S A BIG DIFFERENCE BETWEEN... NEARLY RIGHT AND EXACTLY RIGHT.

It's a funny thing about life...
if you refuse to accept
anything but the best,
you'll get it.

WELL DONE IS BETTER
THAN WELL SAID.

Don't listen to activity...
Listen to results.

You only have
three choices in life…
Survive, Succeed
or Surpass.

Amateurs work until
they get it right…
Professionals work until
they can't get it wrong.

FESTIVITIES

Every day is special…
but some are more important.

FESTIVITIES

Passing Patriotism
Patrick Henry shouted,
"give me liberty or give me death."
The next generation shouted,
"give me liberty."
The next generation shouted,
"give me..."
This generation shouts, "ME!!!"

This is the land of the free...
because of the brave.

**HISTORY WAS WRITTEN IN BLOOD. . .
BEFORE IT EVER WAS WRITTEN IN INK.**

If you can't be content with
what you have received…
then be thankful for
what you have escaped.

WHEN YOU WERE BORN…
YOU CRIED AND
THE WORLD REJOICED.
LIVE YOUR LIFE
IN SUCH A MANNER
THAT WHEN YOU DIE…
THE WORLD CRIES
AND YOU REJOICE.

BIRTHDAYS ARE GOOD FOR YOU.
STATISTICS SHOW THAT THE PEOPLE
WHO HAVE THE MOST BIRTHDAYS…
LIVE THE LONGEST.

So many candles...
so little cake.

CHRISTMAS IS NOW...
BECAUSE CHRISTMAS WAS THEN.

HE BECAME
WHAT WE ARE...
SO THAT
WE COULD BECOME
WHAT HE IS.

The Son of God became
the Son of man...
so that the sons of man
could become
the Sons of God.

**INSTEAD OF BEING THANKFUL
WHEN OUR CUP RUNNETH OVER...
TOO MANY OF US PRAY
FOR A BIGGER CUP.**

*With grateful thanksgiving…
Make us able for this table.*

FERVOR

Whoever stumbles,
but falls not quite…
gains a step.

FERVOR

At 211 degrees water is hot.
At 212 degrees it boils.
And with boiling water comes steam.
And steam can power locomotives.
It's that one extra degree
that makes the difference.

The person who wins may have
been counted out several times...
but he just didn't hear the referee.

NOBODY TRIPS OVER MOUNTAINS.
IT'S THE SMALL PEBBLE THAT
CAUSES YOU TO STUMBLE.
PASS ALL THE PEBBLES IN YOUR PATH. . .
AND YOU WILL FIND YOU HAVE
CROSSED THE MOUNTAIN.

Success is another
form of failure...
if we forget
what our priorities are.

IN THE MIDDLE OF ADVERSITY...
LIES OPPORTUNITY.

*Pay attention to
the little things in life…
because in the end…
you'll find out
they were the big things.*

EVERYONE WHO GOT WHERE HE IS. . .
HAD tO BEGIN WHERE HE WAS.

IDEAS ARE FUNNY
LITTLE THINGS…
THEY WON'T WORK
UNLESS YOU DO.

Pain is temporary.
It may last a minute,
or an hour, or a day, or a year.
But eventually it will subside
and something else will take its place.
But if I quit... it will last forever.

NOT TO SPOIL
THE ENDING FOR YOU...
BUT EVERYTHING
WILL BE OKAY!

WE CANNOT BECOME
WHAT WE NEED TO BE...
BY REMAINING WHAT WE ARE.

*"I've missed more than nine thousand
shots in my career.
I've lost more than three hundred games.
And twenty-six times I've been trusted
to take the game-winning shot… and missed.
Throughout my life and my career, I've failed,
and failed… and failed again.
So that's why I succeed."*
Michael Jordan

IF BETTER IS POSSIBLE…
GOOD IS NOT ENOUGH.

Patience is the ability
to let your light shine…
after your fuse has blown.

FLUFF

The more you know…
the more you know you don't know.

FLUFF

A TRULY HAPPY PERSON. . .
IS ONE WHO CAN ENJOY
THE SCENERY ON A DETOUR.

When God puts
a tear in your eye…
it's because He wants
to put a rainbow in your heart.

Worry does not empty
tomorrow of its sorrow…
it empties today of its strength.

128

It's the little things that fret and worry us.
We can dodge an elephant...
but we can't escape a mosquito.

Inspiration (like these Think Spots)
won't last.
Neither will bathing.
That's why I recommend
a daily dose.

WE SHOULD ALWAYS BE GLAD... THAT GOD DOESN'T GIVE US EVERYTHING WE ASK FOR.

Life is like a novel.
It's filled with surprise.
You have no idea
what's going to happen...
until you turn the page.

IF YOU DON'T THINK
EVERY DAY IS
A GOOD DAY...
JUST TRY SKIPPING ONE.

HOW YOU SAY YOUR WORDS...

MATTERS FAR MORE

THAN THE WORDS YOU SAY.

**IN 1945 A SURVIVOR OF
THE BATTLE OF IWO JIMA SAID,
"WE WERE KNOCKED OFF THE RIDGE SIX TIMES...
BUT WE CAME BACK SEVEN."**

A pessimist is one who makes difficulties of his opportunities… and an optimist is one who makes opportunities of his difficulties.

The grand essentials to happiness in this life are... something to do... something to love... and something to hope for.

IT'S NEVER TOO LATE TO BE... WHO YOU MIGHT HAVE BEEN.

Spring has sprung.
Fall has fell.
Summer is here...
and it's hotter than usual.

TROUBLES ARE LIKE UGLY DOGS. . . THEY LOOK WORSE COMING THAN GOING.

Keep life...
Beauty full.

TO GET NOWHERE...
FOLLOW THE CROWD.

Always be curious.
Knowledge will
never seek you...
you must acquire it.

Show me a man with
both feet on the ground...
and I'll show you a man
who can't get his pants on.

YOU ARE THE LIGHT OF THE WORLD...

BATTERIES NOT INCLUDED.

Life gives you the test first...
and the lesson later.

HE WHO CANNOT DANCE...
BLAMES THE FLOOR.

**SQUEEZE the tube SLOWLY. . .
BECAUSE ONCE
the toothpaste IS OUt
It's PREtty HARD to GEt BACK IN.**

Words last forever.

*Whenever you see a turtle
sitting on a fence post…
you know he did not
get there by himself.*

MAYBE BROCCOLI...
DOESN'T LIKE YOU EITHER.

WHEN LIFE HANDS YOU LEMONS...
DON'T MAKE LEMONADE.
JUST THROW THEM BACK
AND ASK FOR
CHOCOLATE CHIP COOKIES.

Quite often when
a person thinks his mind
is getting broader...
it is only his
conscience stretching.

SWALLOWING YOUR PRIDE...

WILL NEVER GIVE YOU INDIGESTION.

Methods are many,
Principles are few;
Methods may change,
Principles never do.

Today's
little moments become...
tomorrow's
precious memories.

**SYMPATHY IS
NEVER WASTED EXCEPT...
WHEN YOU
GIVE IT TO YOURSELF.**

If it's too much to
love your enemy…
just compromise and
forget the knothead.

YOU CAN't CONVINCE A ROOSTER
HE DOESN't KNOW. . .
AS MUCH ABOUT SINGING
AS A MOCKINGBIRD.

For every mile of
bad road you travel...
there are two miles of
ditch you're staying out of.

NOTHING IS MORE THAN
HALF AS GOOD AS IT WOULD BE
IF IT WERE TWICE AS GOOD AS IT IS.
ON THE OTHER HAND...
EVERYTHING IS TWICE AS
GOOD AS IT WOULD BE
IF IT WERE ONLY HALF AS GOOD AS IT IS.

JUST WHEN I GOT USED TO YESTERDAY... ALONG CAME TODAY.

**If you stick
your head in the sand…
you can expect
a kick in the tail.**

LIGHTNING DOES

THE WORK...

THUNDER TAKES

THE CREDIT.

Laugh when you can…
apologize when you should…
let go of what you can't change.

If it can't be fixed
with duct tape…
then you're not
using enough duct tape.

If you stick your nose
into trouble…
your feet are bound
to follow.

TODAY IS THE
TOMORROW...
YOU WORRIED ABOUT YESTERDAY.

You don't get harmony...
when everyone sings the
same note.

If hard work
is the key to success...
most people would
rather pick the lock.

HOW YOU SAY YOUR WORDS... MATTERS FAR MORE THAN THE WORDS YOU SAY.

What if we treated our Bibles
like our cell phones?
Carried it everywhere.
Turned back to get it if we forgot it.
Checked for messages throughout the day.
Used it in case of emergencies.
Spent an hour or more using it every day.

When I'm lying in my casket,
you can say,
"The shell is here...
but the nut is gone."

IF YOU EAT YOUR VEGETABLES
EVERY DAY FOR 80 YEARS...
YOU WILL NOT DIE YOUNG.

DON'T DRIVE LIKE YOU OWN THE ROAD. . .
DRIVE LIKE YOU OWN THE CAR.

THROW KINDNESS AROUND...
LIKE CONFETTI.

You can't get anywhere today...
if you are still
mired down in yesterday.

Whenever you see
a Bible that's falling apart...
you know it belongs to a person who isn't.

HOWEVER GOOD OR BAD A SITUATION IS... IT WILL CHANGE.

CPSIA information can be obtained
at www.ICGtesting.com
Printed in the USA
FFOW03n1702101117
43456782-42127FF